A BEST FRIEND  and 999 Other Things to Make You HaPPY

by NANCY E. KRULIK

SCHOLASTIC

New York   Toronto   London   Auckland   Sydney
Mexico City   New Delhi   Hong Kong

For Alex Burwasser
I wish you happiness always
— NEK

No part of this work may be reproduced in whole or in part, or stored in a retrieval system, or transmitted in any form or by any means, electronic, mechanical, photocopying, recording, or otherwise, without written permission of the publisher. For information regarding permission, write to Scholastic Inc., Attention: Permissions Department, 555 Broadway, New York, NY 10012.

ISBN 0-439-21313-4

Copyright © 2001 by Scholastic Inc.
All rights reserved. Published by Scholastic Inc.
SCHOLASTIC and associated logos are trademarks and/or registered trademarks of Scholastic Inc.

12 11 10 9 8 7 6 5 4 3 2 1   1 2 3 4 5 6/0

Printed in the U.S.A.   40
First Scholastic printing, April 2001

☺ THINGS TO MAKE YOU HAPPY IN SCHOOL

1. PIZZA DAY IN THE CAFETERIA

2. Sharpened pencils

3. A desk near the window

4. Class picnics

5. Not getting hit in the dodgeball game

6. A clean desk

7. Winning the spelling bee

8. Snow days

9. Recess

10. Playing the cymbals in your school band

11. Having an assigned seat next to your best friend

12. D.E.A.R. Time (Drop Everything and Read)

13. A brand-new box of crayons

14. Half days

15. Special visitors

16. Finally memorizing all of your multiplication tables

17. Learning something new

18. After-school play dates

19. Writing your autobiography

20. Becoming friends with the new kid

21. Discovering that your mom

packed your favorite lunch

22. Class parties

23. Science experiments

24. Getting a note from someone special

25. Finding your missing homework

at the bottom of your backpack

26. A day without homework

27. Gymnastics in gym class

28. Finding your long-lost mitten

   in the lost-and-found box

29. Getting the lead in the school play

30. Learning a new language

31. Assemblies

32. Field trips

33. Getting the backseat in the bus

34. The last day before vacation

35. Arriving on the first day of school and finding out

   you have the nicest teacher in the school

36. After-school clubs

37. Picture day

38. A fire drill during your math test

39. Making papier-mâché sculptures in art class

40. Sitting next to the cutest person in school

41. Decorating your book covers

42. A new pencil case

43. A STAR STICKER AT THE TOP OF YOUR PAPER

44. Pens that write in many colors

45. The cracking sound you hear the first time you open a new book

46. A clean, fresh sheet of paper

47. Big packs of scented markers

48. Hot-pink highlighters

49. When the whole class laughs at your joke

50. Being picked to run an errand for the teacher

51. A new backpack

52. Key chain collections on your backpack

53. Learning to write in cursive

54. Finishing your homework before dinner

55. The very last day of school

☺ THINGS TO MAKE YOU HAPPY AT RECESS

56. Making it all the way without stopping in hopscotch

57. Playing tag . . . and never being "it"

58. A chance to talk to friends who aren't in your class

59. Running, running, running!

60. Hanging upside down

61. Finally mastering jumping double Dutch

62. Chalk pictures on the blacktop

63. SHOOTING HOOPS

64. Getting to watch movies on rainy days

65. The world's biggest dodgeball game

5

☺ THINGS TO MAKE YOU HAPPY AT THE MALL

66. The food court

67. Air-conditioning in the summer

68. Heat in the winter

69. Window-shopping

70. Spending your allowance money

71. Tons of stores

72. Trying on hats

73. NEW JEANS

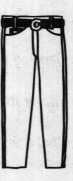

74. Hanging out with your friends

75. Going to the movies

76. Sales

77. Buying presents

78. Lots of shopping bags

79. New stores opening

80. Trying on makeup

81. Escalators

82. Indoor gardens

83. No smoking allowed

84. Being sprayed with perfume

85. Gumball machines

86. Making funny faces in a photo booth

87. Samples from the chocolate shop

88. Flower shows in the spring

89. Great holiday window displays

90. Spending hours in the bookstore

91. Shopping inside while it rains outside

92. Getting a new hairstyle

☺ THINGS TO MAKE YOU HAPPY AT THE THEATER

93. Watching the curtain go up

94. Live actors

95. A real orchestra

96. CHOCOLATE BARS AT INTERMISSION

97. Standing ovations

98. Collecting autographs after the show

99. Velvet seats

100. Reading the program front to back

101. Singing songs from the show as you leave the theater

102. Watching the action through binoculars

☺ THINGS TO MAKE YOU HAPPY AT THE MOVIES

103. Knowing the answers to the on-screen quiz before the movie

104. BUTTERED POPCORN

105. Big sodas

106. Candy you never get at home

107. No one sitting in the seat in front of you

108. Coming attractions

109. Your favorite actor

110. Your favorite actress

111. Laughing out loud

112. Crying in the dark where no one can see you

113. Sneak previews

114. Sitting with friends in a different row from your parents

115. Being the first one in your class to see a new movie

116. The soundtrack

117. Admiring the clothes the actors wear in the movie

118. Big, soft chairs that rock back and forth

119. Cup holders on every seat

120. Extra scenes that play while the credits are running

121. Stadium seating

122. No annoying commercials

123. No phone calls interrupting the best part

124. 3-D glasses

125. Giant IMAX screens

126. Ordering your tickets over the phone

127. Holding hands

☺ THINGS TO MAKE YOU HAPPY AT AN AMUSEMENT PARK

128. Going upside down on the roller coaster

129. Giant costume characters

130. Water rides with big splashes

131. Cotton candy

132. Getting stuck at the top of the Ferris wheel

133. Slamming into your big brother's bumper car

134. Haunted houses

135. Funhouse mirrors

136. Winning a stuffed animal

137. Parades

138. Being tall enough to ride everything

139. Getting your favorite color horse

      on the merry-go-round

140. Mimes

141. No line for your favorite ride

142. Jumping into a ball pit

143. Giant mazes

144. The "Guess Your Age" guy

145. No More Kiddie Rides!

146. FOOT-LONG HOT DOGS

147. Taking funny pictures

148. Making new friends in line

149. The tunnel of love

☺ THINGS TO MAKE YOU HAPPY WHEN YOU WATCH TV

150. Being in charge of the remote

151. BIG-SCREEN TVS

152. Reruns of your favorite shows

153. Knowing the answer before the

game show contestant does

154. A show the whole family likes

155. Funny commercials

156. 100 channels

157. Remembering to tape your favorite

show when you're not home

158. TV game shows you can play along

with on the Internet

159. Old black-and-white movies

160. Sports on TV

161. Special permission to stay up late until a show is over

162. Animal shows

163. Green Nickelodeon slime

164. The Superbowl

165. Imitating the stars' voices

166. Awesome theme songs

☺ THINGS TO MAKE YOU HAPPY AT THE ZOO AND THE AQUARIUM

167. Local squirrels that hang out with

the exotic animals

168. Petting the animals at the children's zoo

169. Seeing animals from faraway places

170. Saving endangered species

171. Making animal noises

172. Walking through a rain forest environment

173. Baby animals

174. Waving to the divers who feed the fish

175. Sharks safely behind glass

176. Seals with balls on their noses

☺ THINGS TO MAKE YOU HAPPY WHEN YOU'RE SICK

177. A warm comforter

178. Candy-flavored medicine

179. Chicken soup

180. Get-well-soon cards

181. Phone calls from friends

182. Word-search puzzles

183. Mom and Dad taking care of you

184. Naps

185. Game shows on TV

186. Feeling better

187. CUDDLY TEDDY BEARS

188. Playing games with Grandma

189. A kiss from your dog

190. Magazines

191. Breakfast in bed

192. Old movies

193. Long baths

194. Laptop computers

195. The fever going down

196. Nurses who make you smile

197. Missing a pop quiz at school

198. Warm stethoscopes

199. As much ice cream as you can eat

200. Throat lozenges

201. Hot tea with honey and lemon

202. No shots!

203. Ear thermometers

204. No wait at the doctor's office

205. Colorful, glow-in-the-dark bandages

206. LOLLIPOPS FROM THE DOCTOR

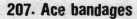

207. Ace bandages

208. Having your friends sign your cast

209. Crutches

210. Extra attention

☺ THINGS TO MAKE YOU HAPPY ABOUT SPORTS

211. Fun teammates

212. Cool uniforms

213. Parent-child softball games

214. BASEBALL CAPS

215. Hitting a home run

216. Catching the ball

217. A new soccer ball

218. Being the goalkeeper

219. Heading the ball to your teammate

220. Wearing the same shoes as your favorite player

221. Snacks at halftime

222. Your own hockey stick

223. Wooden backboards

224. Hearing the basketball "swish"

225. The perfect tennis serve

226. A really close match

227. Being chosen first for the team

228. Cleats

229. Scoring a touchdown

230. FOOTBALL HELMETS

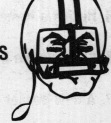

231. Being a good winner

232. A cheering crowd

233. Having friends in the crowd

234. Team pictures

235. Good sportsmanship

236. Trophies

237. Playing your best

☺ THINGS TO MAKE YOU HAPPY ON VACATION

238. Headphones on the plane

239. Little bags of peanuts or pretzels

240. Travel versions of your favorite games

241. The window seat

242. Playing the license-plate game

243. French fries at truck stops

244. Someone else making your bed

245. Breakfast at a restaurant

246. Making new friends

247. Taking pictures of famous places

248. Buying souvenirs

249. Little soaps and shampoos

250. Seeing new places

251. Singing along with the car radio

252. SENDING POSTCARDS TO YOUR FRIENDS

253. Trying new foods

254. Buying lunch from a street vendor

255. Being the stranger in town

256. Relaxing

257. Being the first one on the tour bus

258. Stuffing your suitcase so full you have to sit on it to get it closed

259. A warm-weather vacation when it's cold at home

260. Resort camps for kids

261. Learning to play golf with Dad

262. Being cozy under a blanket in the backseat while Mom drives at night

263. Making memories

264. SNORKLING IN THE OCEAN

265. Trying to speak the language

266. Reading guidebooks

267. Stamps on your passport

268. Setting up your tent at a campsite

269. Eating the fish you caught yourself

270. Finally getting the fire lit after 51 tries

271. Crawling into your sleeping bag after a long day

272. Keeping a vacation journal

273. Seeing your first Broadway show

274. When your little brother finally falls asleep in the car

275. Perfect zoo weather

276. Sunbathing on a big beach towel

277. Getting to see the cockpit

278. Meeting the pilot

279. Looking down at the clouds

280. Food that comes in little trays

281. Riding through tunnels

282. READING A MAP

283. Meeting the train conductor

284. Sleeping on the train

285. Swimming in the hotel pool

286. Checking the globe to see where

you want to go next

287. Going over bridges

288. When the answer to "Are we

there yet?" is "Yes"

289. Collecting matchbooks from different

restaurants around the country

290. Seeing natural wonders

291. Waterfalls and nature trails

292. Ordering room service

293. Horseback riding on the beach

294. Looking at photos when you get home

☺ THINGS TO MAKE YOU HAPPY
AT THE PARK

295. Trees

23

296. Grass

297. Feeding the pigeons

298. No cars

299. A safe place to ride your bike

300. Quiet spots to read

301. Toy boat races

302. Ducks in the pond

303. Twilight concerts in the park

304. Storytellers

305. SQUIRRELS

306. Dogs playing fetch

307. Frisbee golf

308. Climbing on the rocks

309. Birds building nests

310. Outdoor theaters

311. A game of hackey sack

312. Sunshine

313. No sidewalks

314. Park rangers

315. Babies in strollers

316. Playgrounds

317. Rose gardens

☺ THINGS TO MAKE YOU HAPPY AT SUMMER CAMP

318. The top bunk

319. Free swim time

320. Coed socials

321. Food fights

322. Eating in the mess hall

323. LETTERS FROM HOME

324. Care packages

325. Friends from different states

326. Color war

327. Arts and crafts

328. Tennis tournaments

329. Playing tricks on the counselors

330. Camp songs

331. Writing new words to the camp song

332. Sing-alongs by the campfire

333. The camp bus

334. Trading clothes with your cabin mates

335. Late-night ghost stories

336. Camp-outs under the stars

337. Learning to pitch a tent

338. S'mores

339. Horseback-riding lessons

340. Rowboats

341. The nature shack

342. Your first kiss

343. Hikes deep into the woods

344. Collecting autographs on your camp T-shirt

345. Reading by flashlight

346. Bunk-hopping

347. Cool August nights

348. Making shadow puppets on the

side of the tent

349. Visiting Day

350. Packing your suitcase

351. CANOEING

352. Challenging other camps to softball games

353. Tie-dying

354. Sunsets over the lake

355. Picking a cabin name

356. Rowing to the island in the middle of the lake

357. A perfect 10 at inspection

358. Laundry day

359. Getting all your socks back

     from the camp laundry

360. Moonlight swims

361. Rest hour

362. Candy at the canteen

363. Wild animals in the nature shack

364. Camp is not school

365. Getting the lead in the camp play

366. "See ya next summer!"

☺ THINGS TO MAKE YOU HAPPY ABOUT MUSIC

367. A NEW CD PLAYER

368. The car stereo

369. Your first outdoor rock concert

370. Applause at your piano recital

371. Writing your own songs

372. A great new CD

373. Hearing the song you requested on the radio

374. Radio DJs who don't talk a lot

375. Dance CDs

376. The newest dance craze

377. Drum solos

378. Playing the water glasses at dinner

379. Learning to whistle

29

380. Marching bands

381. Wind chimes

382. Harmonicas

383. Canaries singing

384. The Nutcracker Suite

385. Music boxes

386. Player pianos

387. Karaoke machines

388. Singing in the chorus

389. Scary background music at the movies

390. The way your voice sounds when you're in the shower

391. MTV

392. Making your own music video

393. Catchy commercial jingles

394. Carousel music

395. Organ music at the baseball park

396. Everyone standing for the

   "Star-Spangled Banner"

397. Steel-drum street performers

398. Kazoo bands

399. The theme song from your favorite TV show

400. Going caroling

401. Singing in the talent show

☺ **THINGS TO MAKE YOU HAPPY
IN A RESTAURANT**

402. Little packs of sugar

403. Going out to eat with friends

404. Cloth napkins

405. Straws wrapped in paper

406. So many choices

31

407. Getting dressed up for dinner

408. Kids' meals with toys

409. Someone else washing the dishes

410. Using your math skills to add up the check

411. The dessert menu

412. Red drinks with little paper umbrellas in them

413. Waiters and waitresses

414. Crayons on the table and paper tablecloths to draw on

415. Eating by candlelight

416. Food from other countries

☺ THINGS TO MAKE YOU HAPPY ABOUT YOUR COMPUTER

417. E-mail from friends

418. Music web sites

419. New games to play

420. On-line celebrity chats

421. A new computer table

422. Typing your book report

423. A faster modem

424. Buddy lists

425. Graphic arts

426. Cut-and-paste

427. Spell check

428. Printing in color

429. Knowing things your parents don't

430. On-line shopping

431. Your very own laptop

432. Photos on disks

433. Search engines

434. All the research material you need

435. Communicating with people all over the world

436. More, more, more memory

437. Scanners

438. Funny dot-com TV commercials

439. Computers in all different colors

440. Making cool party invitations

with your drawing program

441. Digital cameras

☺ THINGS TO MAKE YOU HAPPY AT THE LIBRARY

442. THOUSANDS OF BOOKS TO CHOOSE FROM

443. Quiet

444. Your own library card

445. Finishing your report

446. Couches to read on

447. Reading new books for free

448. Videos to borrow

449. Book club meetings

450. Finding just the right book

451. The flowers on the librarian's desk

452. Renewing a book so you can read it again

453. Finally figuring out the Dewey

decimal system

☺ THINGS TO MAKE YOU HAPPY AT A SLEEPOVER

454. Sleeping bags

455. Whispering in the night

456. Scary movies

457. Not sleeping at all

458. Raiding the refrigerator

459. Doing each other's hair

460. Giggling

461. Painting each other's nails

462. Pancakes for breakfast

463. Funny pajamas

464. Stuffed animals

☺ THINGS TO MAKE YOU HAPPY ABOUT YOUR COLLECTIONS AND HOBBIES

465. A rare baseball card

466. Trading with your friends

467. Protective plastic card holders

468. **STAMPS FROM OTHER COUNTRIES**

469. Having all the books in a series

470. Conventions

471. Finally getting all fifty of the state quarters

472. A rock with a fossil in it

473. Flying your model airplane

474. Finishing the ship in a bottle

475. Building a model car

476. Spotting a bird you've never seen before

477. Using your new camera

478. Winning at the art show

479. Perfecting a new magic trick

480. Wearing the scarf you knitted yourself

☺ THINGS TO MAKE YOU HAPPY ON YOUR BIRTHDAY

481. Planning a party

482. Sending out invitations

483. RSVPs that say "Yes"

484. Blowing out all the candles on your cake

485. Making a secret wish

486. Candles that won't blow out

487. Decorations

488. BEAUTIFUL CAKES

489. Being one year closer to your driver's license

490. Being the center of attention

491. Birthday cards in the mail

492. Phone calls from relatives

493. The "Happy Birthday" song

494. All your favorite foods for dinner

495. Cupcakes at school

496. Noisemakers

497. Snacks

498. Balloons

499. Birthday breakfasts

500. "Surprise!"

501. Ripping off the wrapping paper

502. Presents

503. All your friends together

504. Birthday spankings

505. Looking at pictures of yourself

from the day you were born

506. Enough icing roses for everyone

☺ THINGS TO MAKE YOU HAPPY WHEN YOU GET BRACES

507. Rubber bands in cool colors

508. Straight teeth

509. Finding your lost retainer

510. A really cool night-brace

511. Cement molds of your teeth

512. Orthodontist chairs that go up and down

513. Drinking a soothing, cold milk shake

after your appointment

514. Adults with braces

515. Feeling your teeth when the

braces finally come off

516. A beautiful smile

☺ THINGS TO MAKE YOU HAPPY AT THE MUSEUM

517. Sketch pads to practice your drawing

518. Colored pencils

519. Famous paintings

520. Imitating the statues' poses

521. Buying postcard versions of the paintings

522. Old-fashioned costumes

523. Hands-on displays

524. Statues with no heads

525. Meeting real artists

526. Children's museums

527. Looking for different shapes in

abstract paintings

528. Mummies

529. Taking art classes in the museum

530. Tossing coins into the fountain

531. GIANT DINOSAURS

532. Planetarium space shows

☺ THINGS TO MAKE YOU HAPPY ABOUT YOUR PET

533. Warm, furry cuddles

534. Long walks together

535. Watching your cat nap in the sun

536. Fancy leashes and collars

537. Hamster wheels

538. Wet licks on your cheek

539. It can't talk back

540. Companionship

541. Happy greetings at the door

542. Wagging tails

543. Feeling protected

544. Talking birds

545. Singing with your canary

546. Meowing at each other

547. PICKING OUT THE PERFECT PUPPY

548. Teaching your parrot to say its name

549. Surprise! Your guinea pig had babies!

550. Someone to sneak food to under the table

551. Picking a name for your pet

552. Watching your goldfish swim in and out of the castle

553. Scratching your cat behind the ears

554. Wet splashy dog baths

555. Throwing sticks into the water

556. A new squeaky toy for your dog's birthday

557. A catnip mouse for your cat

558. A treat stick for your parakeet

559. Doggie booties and raincoats

560. Counting the spots on your dalmatian

561. It's not your turn to clean the litter box

562. Dog runs in the city

563. SCARING PEOPLE WITH YOUR SNAKE

564. Puppies that chase their tails

☺ THINGS TO MAKE YOU HAPPY
ON FIELD TRIPS

565. Being outside on a school day

566. Tour guides

567. Being partners with your best friend

568. Chatting all day long

569. Singing on the bus

570. A change in your everyday schedule

571. Boxed lunches from the cafeteria

572. Hands-on learning

573. No desks for the day!

☺ THINGS TO MAKE YOU HAPPY
ON PLAY DATES

574. Someone else's games

575. Your friend's really nice parents

44

576. Calling home when you get there

577. DIFFERENT SNACKS THAN YOU HAVE AT HOME

578. Playing games

579. Doing homework together

580. Biking

581. Dancing to CDs

582. Putting on a show for the baby-sitter

583. Three friends all getting along

584. Letting a little brother play, too

☺ THINGS TO MAKE YOU HAPPY ON THE WEEKEND

585. Going to the beach

586. Staying up late

587. Sleeping late

588. Wearing old T-shirts

589. Helping with the gardening

590. Kicking back and relaxing

591. Big breakfasts

592. No homework

593. Pickup basketball games

594. Family time

595. Early-morning cartoons

596. Visits from Grandma

597. Mom and Dad relaxing

598. The smell of fresh-cut grass

599. No rushing to get out of the house in the morning

600. Spending the whole day at the playground or the pool

☺ THINGS TO MAKE YOU HAPPY ON RAINY DAYS

601. Counting the seconds between the lightning

    and the thunder to see how far away the storm is

602. The whole family hanging out together

603. A chance to do art projects

604. Spending time on-line

605. Curling up with a good book

606. Talking on the phone for hours

607. Watching raindrops slide down the window

608. Tracing raindrops onto paper

609. The sound of the rain on the roof

610. Knowing the rain is helping the trees and flowers

611. Lots of TV

612. Indoor picnics with no ants

613. Great old movies

614. Yellow rain slickers

615. Rain boots

616. Playing in the mud

617. Washing your hair in the rain

618. Catching rainwater in a barrel

619. Rainbows

☺ THINGS TO MAKE YOU HAPPY WITH YOUR PARENTS

620. Good-night kisses

621. Someone to push you on the swings

622. Shoulders to cry on

623. The perfect people to review your homework

624. Someone to trust with your secrets

625. Cooking together

626. Family jokes

627. Letting them use your nickname

628. Eating in the dining room for no reason

629. Creating your own family traditions

630. Code words only your family knows

631. Family vacations

632. Their big bed

633. People who are (almost) always in your corner

634. Calling them your 'rents

635. Carpool chauffeurs

636. Using their office copy machines

637. Catching Mom and Dad stealing a kiss

638. Hearing them say, "I'm proud of you."

639. Feeling safe when they're around

640. Family game nights

641. The surprise gifts they bring back
from business trips

642. Watching them get all dressed up

643. Bear hugs

644. Feeling all cozy in one of Dad's sweaters

645. Walking around the house in Mom's high heels

☺ THINGS TO MAKE YOU HAPPY
WITH YOUR GRANDPARENTS

646. Hearing stories about your mom when she was
your age

647. Hearing stories about your dad when he was
your age

648. Secret family recipes

649. Unexpected gifts

650. Old-fashioned music on the stereo

651. Being spoiled

652. BAKING COOKIES

653. An old-fashioned home-movie projector

654. Learning to knit

655. Long walks around the neighborhood

656. Hearing stories about the old days

when they were growing up

657. Pictures of Grandma and Grandpa

when they were kids

658. Unlimited kisses and hugs

659. Being around people who think

you're the greatest

660. Coins jingling in Grandpa's pockets

661. Homemade apple pie

☺ THINGS TO MAKE YOU HAPPY WITH YOUR BROTHERS AND SISTERS

662. A permanent playmate

663. Getting advice that you need

664. Giving advice that helps

665. Love

666. Fighting, but knowing you'll always make up

667. Someone to hang out with at

boring family gatherings

668. Bunk beds

669. Cool hand-me-down clothes

670. Toys to share

671. Pillow fights

672. Playing games together in the backseat of the car

☺ THINGS TO MAKE YOU HAPPY IN YOUR HOUSE

673. Long talks in the kitchen

674. Toys in the playroom

675. Everyone reading in the living room

676. A funky new shower curtain

677. Your own room

678. Parties in the basement

679. Sliding down the stairs

680. Knowing Mom and Dad are in the next room

681. Hiding in the hall closet

682. Your own backyard

683. Everyone's radio playing different

channels at the same time

684. Guests in the guest room

685. A new bike in the garage

686. The sunroom filled with plants

687. The tools at your father's workbench

688. Your own tree house

689. Your first set of house keys

690. A+ spelling tests on the refrigerator

691. The whole family watching

the same TV show

692. A doggie door

693. A birdhouse in the yard

694. Eating veggies that came from your

own garden

695. An address that belongs only to your family

☺ THINGS TO MAKE YOU HAPPY IN YOUR ROOM

696. Sheets that match the comforter

697. A favorite stuffed animal

698. Movie star posters

699. The radio tuned to your station

700. Full bookshelves

701. A door you can close when you

want to be alone

702. Your own window

703. CDs that you like

704. A junk drawer

705. A secret place for your diary

706. The mess under your bed

707. An unmade bed

708. Photos of your family

709. Pictures of your friends

710. Lots of clothes in the closet

711. A full-length mirror on your closet door

712. Dancing in front of the mirror

713. A teddy bear collection

☺ THINGS TO MAKE YOU HAPPY WITH YOUR FRIENDS

714. People to sit with at lunch

715. Someone to talk to about your secret crush

716. Trips to the mall

717. Total honesty

718. Friendship bracelets

719. Study groups

720. Sleepover parties

721. Jokes

722. All-night movie marathons

723. Truth or dare

724. Someone with whom you can share
your dreams

725. Exchanging valentines

726. Playing "Heart and Soul" together
on the piano

727. Secret languages and codes

728. Pinky swearing

729. Singing

730. Bicycles built for two

731. Taffy pulls

732. Doing jigsaw puzzles together

733. Someone to call for an answer on a crossword puzzle

734. Wearing matching baseball caps

735. Starting a club

736. Sharing an umbrella

737. Jumping rope at the same time

738. Sharing a seat on the bus

739. Walking to school together

740. Playing a game of catch

741. Someone to practice soccer with

742. Staying on the phone while

you watch the same TV show

743. A secret knock

744. One soda and two straws

745. Borrowing CDs

746. Knowing the perfect birthday present to buy

747. Someone to keep you company

while you wait in line at the movies

748. Saying "cheers" with your soda glasses

749. A great best friend

750. Traveling in a crowd of friends

751. Doing a school project together

752. Eating at your best friend's house for dinner

753. Best-friend necklaces

754. Late-night e-mails

755. Being on the same side in tug-of-war

756. Practicing dance steps with the

perfect partner

☺ THINGS TO MAKE YOU HAPPY IN THE CITY

757. Lots of restaurants

59

758. Museums

759. Riding the bus

760. Underground subway trains

761. Elevated trains

762. Clothing boutiques

763. Spotting famous stars on the street

764. Flea markets

765. Hailing a taxi

766. Visiting places you've seen in the movies

767. Pizza deliveries

768. Street fairs

769. Broadway theater

770. Street performers

771. Double-decker tour buses

772. Police officers on horseback

773. Tourists

774. Firefighters who wave to you

775. Riding in a horse and carriage

776. Doormen

777. Huge apartment buildings

778. People who walk really, really fast

779. Hot-dog vendors

☺ THINGS TO MAKE YOU HAPPY IN THE SUBURBS

780. Backyard swing sets

781. Lots of kids around

782. Carpools

783. Neighborhood swim clubs

784. Really nice neighbors

785. Convenience stores

786. School carnivals

787. Cul-de-sacs

788. BACKYARD BARBECUES

☺ THINGS TO MAKE YOU HAPPY IN THE COUNTRY

789. Fresh air

790. LEARNING TO MILK A COW

791. Haystacks

792. Rows and rows of tall corn

793. Crickets chirping at night

794. Fresh eggs

795. No traffic

796. Old dirt roads

797. Newborn pink piglets

798. Riding on a tractor

799. Scarecrows

800. Feeding a horse an apple

801. Secret places you can be alone

☺ THINGS TO MAKE YOU HAPPY
IN THE WINTER

802. Going sledding

803. Icicles hanging from the trees

804. Holidays

805. Presents with big bows

806. Packages that come in the mail from far away

807. Chestnuts roasting

808. Motorized holiday decorations in the store windows

809. Letters to Santa Claus

810. Hanging stockings

811. CANDLES FOR KWANZA

812. Candy canes

813. The dreidel game

814. Learning how to snowboard

815. Bunny slopes at the ski hill

816. Riding the ski lift

817. Snow angels

818. Snowball fights

819. Snow forts

820. Not slipping on the ice

821. Mini-marshmallows in your hot chocolate

822. Hot soup

823. Cuddling with your dog

824. A car that warms up quickly

825. Catching snowflakes on your tongue

826. Thick socks

827. Warm boots

828. A new sweater

829. School vacation

830. Making paper snowflakes

831. Gingerbread cookies

832. Building a snowman

833. Saving snowballs in the freezer

834. Visits from family

835. Big scarves

836. Neon-colored ski pants

837. Frozen ponds to skate on

838. Going ice fishing

839. NEW YEAR'S PARTY HATS

840. Roses, candy, and kisses for Valentine's Day

841. Getting lots of valentines

842. Heart candies with words on them

843. The wind howling outside

844. Long underwear

845. A hat for your snowman

846. Pretending to be a polar bear

847. Footprints in fresh snow

848. Fireplaces

849. Ice hockey

850. Basketball games

851. Indoor heated pools

852. Millions of different snowflakes

853. Down parkas

854. Hats that cover your whole face

855. New skates

856. Perfect snowball snow

857. Finally getting your figure eight right

858. Starting a snow-shoveling business

859. Funny ear muffs

860. Fuzzy slippers

861. Electric blankets

☺ THINGS TO MAKE YOU HAPPY IN THE SPRING

862. FRESH FLOWERS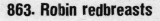

863. Robin redbreasts

864. Green grass

865. Playing outside without a coat

866. Baseball season

867. Fresh air

868. Playing Frisbee

869. Rolling down a grassy hill

870. Kites

871. April showers

872. May flowers

873. Singing in the rain

874. Jumping in puddles

875. BUNNIES

876. Jellybeans

877. Easter egg hunts

878. June weddings

879. The NBA championships

880. Daylight saving time

881. Leaves budding on the trees

882. Jumping rope

883. Spring fever

884. Planting a garden

885. Rope swings

886. Short sleeves

887. Rosy cheeks

888. Sweet smells in the air

889. BUTTERFLIES

890. In-line skates

☺ THINGS TO MAKE YOU HAPPY IN THE SUMMER

891. Grass between your toes

892. Sandals

893. Outdoor swimming pools

894. Sprinklers

895. No homework for two months!

896. Camp

897. Cool shade under a tree

898. Sunshine

899. Sun showers

900. Campfires

901. Toasted marshmallows

902. CHERRY POPSICLES

903. Chewing ice cubes

904. Going to a baseball game

905. The music of the ice-cream truck

906. Wading in the river

907. Going rafting

908. Rainbows

909. Outdoor concerts

910. Shorts and T-shirts

911. Building sand castles

912. Riding the waves

913. Collecting seashells

914. Burying your dad in the sand

915. Canoe trips

916. Diving

917. Lawn furniture

918. A new bathing suit

919. Sailing

920. Waterskiing

921. Splashing your friends

922. Handheld fans

923. Beach volleyball

924. Catching fireflies . . . and setting them free

925. The sun staying up until late

926. Drive-in movies

927. Water bottles at the tennis courts

928. Lying around and staring at the pictures in the clouds

929. Relay races

930. Hikes in the woods

931. Water-gun battles

932. Picnic baskets

933. Ceiling fans

934. COLD LEMONADE

935. Barbecue sauce

936. Fireworks on the Fourth of July

937. Golf

938. Air-conditioning in the car

939. Plastic ice cubes that look like fruit

940. Playing the guitar under a tree

941. Going fishing

942. Making grass whistles

943. Water balloons

944. Open fire hydrants

945. Swimming holes

946. Blue skies

947. Soda in the cooler

948. Long bike rides

949. Listening to the ocean in a seashell

950. Saltwater taffy

951. Walking on the boardwalk

952. Beach blankets

953. The smell of sunscreen

954. The smell of the ocean

955. Boogie boarding

956. Cannonballs off the diving board

957. Being brave enough to jump off the high dive

958. Underwater handstands

959. Chicken fights in the pool

☺ THINGS TO MAKE YOU HAPPY IN THE FALL

960. Beautiful colors on the trees

961. Leaves crackling beneath your feet

962. Jumping in piles of leaves

963. Hayrides

964. Picking apples

965. Sweater weather

966. The colors in Indian corn

967. PUMPKIN PATCHES

968. Jack-o'-lanterns

969. Witches, ghosts, and goblins

970. Trick or treat

971. New school clothes

972. Seeing old friends after the long summer

973. Hot cider with cinnamon sticks

974. Pumpkin pie

975. New TV shows

976. Scary movies

977. Earlier sunsets

978. Later sunrises

979. Bird formations as they fly south

980. Frost on the grass

981. A season with two names—fall and autumn

982. The World Series

983. Football season

984. New friends at school

985. Candy corn

986. The harvest moon

987. BLACK CATS

988. Turkey and stuffing

989. Families saying thanks

990. Acting out the first Thanksgiving

991. Cranberries

992. Leftover turkey on rye bread

993. Jean jackets

994. Bird feeders

995. Watching the squirrels collect nuts in their cheeks

996. Saying good-bye to daylight saving time

997. Street hockey games

998. Touch football games

999. Making a compost pile

1000. Fog coming out of your mouth when you breathe